YOUR KNOWLEDGE HAS VALUE

- We will publish your bachelor's and master's thesis, essays and papers

- Your own eBook and book - sold worldwide in all relevant shops

- Earn money with each sale

Upload your text at www.GRIN.com and publish for free

Bibliographic information published by the German National Library:

The German National Library lists this publication in the National Bibliography; detailed bibliographic data are available on the Internet at http://dnb.dnb.de .

Imprint:

Copyright © 2017 GRIN Verlag, Open Publishing GmbH
Print and binding: Books on Demand GmbH, Norderstedt Germany
ISBN: 9783668461017

This book at GRIN:

http://www.grin.com/en/e-book/366677/biomedical-waste-management

Pyali Chatterjee

Biomedical waste management

GRIN Publishing

GRIN - Your knowledge has value

Since its foundation in 1998, GRIN has specialized in publishing academic texts by students, college teachers and other academics as e-book and printed book. The website www.grin.com is an ideal platform for presenting term papers, final papers, scientific essays, dissertations and specialist books.

Visit us on the internet:

http://www.grin.com/

http://www.facebook.com/grincom

http://www.twitter.com/grin_com

MEDICAL SCIENCE IS FOR THE ERADICATION OF ILLNESS FROM THE SOCIETY AND NOT FOR SPREADING HAZARDUS SUBTANCES IN THE SOCIETY

PYALI CHATTERJEE

Phd Scholar, Amity University, Noida, India

Contents

1. INTRODUCTION

The issue of Biomedical Waste was discussed first in International level by World Health Organization, Regional Office of Europe in the year 1983 at Bergen , Norway[1].

When we talked about environmental pollution, we know that many kinds waste products were generated from Industries sectors, automobiles sectors, Medicals/ Nursing homes and from our homes etc that caused pollution in the air, water and land and spread diseases like Asthma, Hepatitis B and C, jaundice, malaria etc. Even though Government has framed different polices to control the every kind pollution but still somewhere due to the loopholes in law, we fail to control pollution.

Due to modernization and a fast growing population , life of peoples become so busy and hectic that no one is concerned for the health of others. Moreover, even sometimes knowingly or unknowingly we try to avoid circumstances, which can cause great danger to our life as well as to others also. And one of such danger is biomedical hazards.

Whenever we get ill, we use to run to the hospitals for treatment. And for diagnosis certain test is conducted or sometimes we get hospitalize. But ever we tried to enquire about the different types of wastes which are daily generated from the hospitals or who are the staffs who handle these biomedical waste products. And how much this biomedical waste can be dangerous to human beings and also to the environment. And how this waste is treated before dumping and where they dumped it.

The Honorable Supreme Court of India in Dr. B.L. Wadehra versus Union of India and Others, (1996) 2SCC 594, has discussed about the different types of waste generated from the Industries and Hospitals and how they were treated. In this case, Supreme Court said that it is the constitutional right of the citizen to have pollution free air, water and to live in a clean city[2]. In addition, certain direction were even given to the Municipal Corporation of Delhi and New Delhi Municipal Council for the management of solid waste including biomedical waste.

---

[1] Sacchidananda Mukherjee and Debasis Chakraborty," Environmental Scenario in India: Successes and Predicaments" (Abingdon: Routledge, 2012), 189
[2] Dr. P.S. Jaswal and Dr. Nishtha Jaswal,"Enviromental Law"3rd Edn,(Faridabad: Allahabad Law Agency,2009),169

And it was after this case, The Bio-Medical Waste (Management and Handling) Rules, 1998 was enacted on 27th July 1998 under Environment Protection Act, 1986.

Today biomedical waste has become a great concern for the entire environmentalist in the world. Because most of us, use to neglect this issue even though we are aware of the fact that how much it is dangerous, infectious and nuisance. Moreover, the way they are treated, handled and dumped without following the rules mentioned under The Bio-Medical Waste (Management and Handling) Rules, 1998 are more dangerous to life and environment

2. DEFINITION OF BIOMEDICAL WASTE

"Biomedical waste, also known as infectious waste or medical waste is defined as solid waste generated during the diagnosis, testing, treatment, research or production of biological products for humans or animals. Biomedical waste includes syringes, live vaccines, laboratory samples, body parts, bodily fluids and waste, sharp needles, cultures and lancets.[3]"

And according to the definition given in the Bio-Medical Waste (Management and Handling) Rules, 1998

"Bio- medical waste means any waste, which is generated during the diagnosed, treatment or immunization of human beings or animals or in research activities pertaining thereto or in the production or testing of biological.[4]"

2.1 CATAGORIES OF BIOMEDICAL HAZARDS

As per Rule.4 of The Bio-Medical Waste (Management and Handling) Rules, 1998, "it shall be the duty of the "occupier[5]" of an institution generating biomedical waste to take

---

[3] Yamini Ugender, "Biomedical Waste Definition", eHow Contributor,
http://www.ehow.com/about_5452204_biomedical-waste-definition.html(accessed August 21, 2014)

[4] Bio-Medical Waste (Management and Handling) Rules, 1998 http://envfor.nic.in/legis/hsm/biomed.html (accessed August 21, 2014)

[5] Ibid., See.Rule 3(4) for definition of Occupier

all steps to ensure that such waste is handled without any adverse effect to human health and the environment"[6].

The category of the biomedical waste is mentioned under Schedule 1 of Rule 5. Rule 5 (1) of The Bio-Medical Waste (Management and Handling) Rules, 1998 says about the manner and way how it should be treated and disposed under Schedule I of the same.(Table.1)

Rule 6 of The Bio-Medical Waste (Management and Handling) Rules, 1998 deals with "Segregation, Packing, Transportation and Storage of the biomedical waste[7]". Rule 6(1), strictly says that the biomedical waste should not be mixed with other waste. Rule 6(2) says that biomedical waste should be segregated first in accordance to Schedule II of the same and that also prior to its storage, transportation, treatment and disposal. In addition, the container should be labeled according to Schedule III. The Chart for Categories of Biomedical Waste is given under Table-1 and the chart for Colour Coding And Type Of Container For Disposal Of Biomedical Wastes is given under Table-2.

TABLE-1

CATEGORIES OF BIOMEDICAL WASTE[8]

Category	Wastes	Treatment
1	**Human Anatomical Waste**(Human tissues, Organs, body parts)	Incineration or deep burial.
2	**Animal Waste** (Animal tissues, organs, body parts, carcasses, bleeding parts, fluid, blood and experimental animals used in research, waste generated by Vetenary hospitals and colleges, discharge from hospitals, animal houses)	Incineration or deep burial.

---

[6] Dr. P.S. Jaswal and Dr. Nishtha Jaswal,"Enviromental Law"3rd Edn,(Faridabad: Allahabad Law Agency,2009),429

[7] Bio-Medical Waste (Management and Handling) Rules, 1998, Rule 6.

http://envfor.nic.in/legis/hsm/biomed.html (accessed August 21, 2014)

[8] Ibid. Schedule I of Rule 5.

3	**Microbiology and biotechnology waste**(waste from laboratory cultures, stocks or specimens of micro-organisms live or attenuated vaccines, human and animal cell culture used in research and infectious agents from research and infectious agents from research and industrial laboratories, waste from production biological, toxins, dishes and devices used for transfer of cultures.	Local autoclaving or microwaving or incineration
4	**Waste sharps** (needles, syringes, scalpels, blades, glass etc. that may cause disinfection, puncture and cuts. This includes both used and unused sharps)	Chemical treatment or autoclaving or microwaving and mutilation/shredding.
5	**Discarded medicines and cyto toxic drugs** (wastes comprising of outdated, contaminated and discarded medicines)	Incineration or destruction and disposal in secured landfills.
6	**Solid waste**(items contaminated with blood and body fluids including cotton, dressing, soiled plaster castes, bedding and other materials contaminated with blood.	Incineration or autoclaving or microwaving.
7	**Solid waste** (wastes generated from disposable items other than the waste sharps such as tubing, catheters, intravenous sets, etc.	Disinfection by chemical treatment or autoclaving or microwaving and mutilation or shredding.
8	**Liquid waste** (waste generated from laboratory and washing, cleaning, housekeeping and the disinfecting activities).	Disinfection by chemical treatment and discharge into drains.
9	**Incineration ash** (ash from incineration	Disposal in municipal landfills.

		of any bio- medical waste)	
10	**Chemical waste** (chemicals used in production of biological, chemicals used in chemical disinfection as insecticides, etc).	Chemical treatment and discharge into drains for liquids and secured land fill for solids.

TABLE-2

COLOUR CODING AND TYPE OF CONTAINER FOR DISPOSAL OF BIOMEDICAL WASTES[9]

Colour Coding of bag	Types of Containers -Waste Type	Treatment option as per Schedule 1 of Rule5
Yellow	**Plastic bags**:-Human Anatomical Waste, Animal waste, Human Anatomical Waste, Animal Waste, Microbiology and Biotechnology waste, Blood contaminated Solid.	Incineration/Deep burial
Red	**Disinfectant Container/Plastic Bag-** Microbiology and biotechnology waste, blood contaminated solid waste, disposable items.	Autoclaving/Microwaving/ Chemical treatment.
Blue/white/translucent	**Plastic Bag/Puncture proof**-Waste Sharps, Disposable items	Autoclaving /Microwaving/Chemical Treatment destruction /Shredding.
Black	**Plastic bag**-Discarded medicines, Incineration ash, Solid chemicals waste	Secured landfill

---

[9] Ibid., Schedule II, Rule 6

7

Even Rule 6(2) says that each container should be labeled according to Schedule III of The Bio-Medical Waste (Management and Handling) Rules, 1998(*Figure.1*)

Schedule III: Label for Bio-Medical Waste Containers/Bags

Figure.1[10]: Schedule III of The Bio-Medical Waste (Management and Handling) Rules, 1998

3. PROBLEMS REALETING TO BIOMEDICAL WASTE

India is the second largest country with high population density. And most of the people lives here under below poverty line. Numbers of peoples are there who even don't have the roof to stay and food to eat also.

And some of the people from this section work as rag pickers. And they can earn money from the rag which we used to through in the garbage. They collect it and used to sell it to the purchaser who used those rags for recycling. These people are more prone to get infection from these kinds of works.

Even though we had a strict Rule to deal with biomedical waste and for its recycling and also for its dumping, but the scenario is very much different which we can find from the below pictures taken by various newspapers etc. and the way it is handled is more dangerous. That we can find from the following photographs.

3.1 DUMPING OF BIOMEDICAL WASTE

---

[10] Praveen Mathur, Sangeeta Patan and Anand S. Shobhawat," Need of Biomedical Waste System in Hospital-An Emerging issue-Review", Current World Environment., Vol.7 (1), 117-124 (2012)

The dumping of biomedical waste has become one of the great concerns for all environmentalists, medical institution and for the Government body also. Since many serious issue is concerned with it relating to health, nuisance and pollution. From time to time and from our surrounding we have found that how the medical institution dumped they are biomedical waste.

One of such incident we can find, where used syringes was dumped near to a compound side of K.P. Vallon Road near Kadavanthara[11]. In this particular case it was found that the disposed syringes were intact with the needles. And according to The Bio-Medical Waste (Management and Handling) Rules, 1998 the used syringes should be treated according to Schedule I of Rule 5. It should be the duty of the medical institution to have nozzle cutter and a needle burner to cut the nozzle of the syringes and also to burn the needles before disposal, so that that nobody can misuse it or reuse it.

In a recent study done by Central Pollution Control Board (CPCB) it is found that fifty percent of the biomedical wastes are treated before it's dumped and the rest is untreated and dumped with municipal garbage[12].

In another case, Nair Hospitals of Mumbai Central[13] used to dump their untreated biomedical waste at the backward of their hospitals. The rag pickers they used to enter into the campus without any interruption from the hospitals authority to collect the rag from the biomedical waste. It was also found that most the biomedical waste was untreated. And it's a rule that the biomedical waste should not be dumped in this way. It should be the duty of the Hospital authority to handle and dumped the biomedical waste in accordance with The Bio-Medical Waste (Management and Handling) Rules, 1998 with proper labeling of biomedical waste hazards symbols.

---

[11] Staff Reporter, "Biomedical waste found dumped in heart of kochi", The Hindu, January 7, 2013 http://www.thehindu.com/news/cities/Kochi/biomedical-waste-found-dumped-in-heart-of-kochi/article4282461.ece (accessed 25 August 2014)

[12] Piyush Diwan," Lack of facilities to treat bio medical waste produced in the country", TopNews.in, April 14, 2010
http://topnews.in/lack-facilities-treat-bio-medical-waste-produced-country-2258794(accessed 28 August 2014)
[13] Swati Jha, "A Dickensian scene at Nair Hospital", The Free Press Journal since 1928, August 6, 2013 http://freepressjournal.in/a-dickensian-scene-at-nair-hospital/(accessed 28 August 2014)

3.2. HEALTH ISSUE

The following are the Health issue related to biomedical waste if it is not handled/managed with proper way[14]:-

1) Hepatitis Band C
2) HIV infection
3) Gastro-enteric infection
4) Respiratory infection
5) Blood Stream infection
6) Skin infection
7) Radioactive toxicity
8) Water and air bore disease

Sharps which is described under Schedule 1 of Rule 5, is to be handled with proper care. As they are the most dangerous carrier of the deadly diseases like Hepatitis B and C and HIV. Moreover, those who handled it with bare hands or without proper care like the hospital staffs and rag pickers are very prone to these diseases.

In a study conducted by WHO in 2000, it was found that near about 21 millions peoples were suffered from Hepatitis B and two million from Hepatitis C and two lakhs sixty thousands from HIV and all because of the infected needles and syringes pricked during scavenging this from dumpsite[15].

Sometimes hospitals authority used to dumped biomedical waste with municipal waste, in that case cattle's and dogs get infected from the biomedical waste which was mixed with municipal waste and sometimes they may died if they consume sharps like needles or broken glass with foods materials from garbage.

In addition, it is also found that, biomedical waste that comes in the Category 1, 2 and 6 of Schedule 1 of Rule 5 of The Bio-Medical Waste (Management and Handling) Rules, 1998 might cause nuisance in the society, if it is not treated and dumped properly.

---

[14] "Health Care Waste Management Scenario In West Bengal"
http://www.wbpcb.gov.in/html/downloads/bmw_report.pdf(accessed 28, August 2014)

[15] "Health-care waste Management", World Health Organization, October 2011
http://www.who.int/mediacentre/factsheets/fs281/en/(accessed 28 August 2014)

3.3. ENVIRONMENT POLLUTION

The process of treating biomedical waste through Incineration is one of the concerns of the Environmentalist, researchers of the entire world. As waste management through incineration is dangerous to environment because of the pollutant, it emits like Dioxins and bottom waste and fly ash, and Dioxins is one of the most toxic gas and it is dangerous to health and environment. In recent years many organization like WHO[16] has done research on Incineration and submitted its report about the dangerous impact of Incineration in the environment and health. Many researchers Like Paul Connett, argued for, to stop use of the Incineration as waste management process[17]. As the process is not only dangerous to health and environment but it is one of the most costly, process of treatment of waste including biomedical waste. The Government should choose some alternative methods for waste management in place of Incineration.

Biomedical waste like blood bags, syringes, fluid bags etc should not be incinerated as it is made up of plastic and plastic contains polyvinyl chloride, which after incineration produced Dioxin etc. So the products, which are made of plastics, should be avoided for the process of Incineration. The International Agency for Research on Cancer (IARC)[18] found that dioxin is one of the major causes of cancer. The exposure to dioxin can cause disease like impairment of immune system and nervous system, endocrine system and the reproductive functions depending upon the exposure to dioxin. Even animals were also found to be suffering from cancer due to its some kind of exposure to dioxin.

The Delhi High Court in **P.K Nayyar and Others Versus UOI and Others and Synergy Waste Management Pvt Ltd versus UOI and Others**[19], asked the Delhi Government and the Synergy Waste management Pvt Ltd to shift the Biomedical Waste

---

[16] Ibid.

[17] Paul Connett, "Why incineration is a very bad idea in the Twenty First Century", Global Anti Incinerator Alliance
http://www.no-burn.org/downloads/Why%20incineration%20is%20a%20very%20bad%20idea%20%20in%20the%20Twenty%20First%20Century.pd f(accessed 28 August 2014)

[18] "Health-care waste Management", World Health Organization, October 2011
http://www.who.int/mediacentre/factsheets/fs281/en/(accessed 28 August 2014)
[19] W.P.(C)NO.6976/2008 and W.P.(C) 5683/2010,
http://www.delhicourts.nic.in/Jan13/P.K.%20Nayyar%20vs.%20UOI.pdf(accessed August 29, 2014)

Management facility from Sukhdev Vihar to some other place. As the Waste Management was close to the residential area and was emitting poisonous gases, causing serious health problem to the residents of Sukhdev Vihar.

According to the guidelines of Central Pollution Control Board, the Common Biomedical Waste Treatment Facility must be situated to a place far from the residential area and to set this facility minimum one-acre land is required. In this case, it was found that, there was a violation of these guidelines. Thus Delhi High Court, asked the Synergy Waste Management to shift its facility.

Even in this case the court discussed about the harmful impact of Incineration in the society[20].

Dr. Ravi Agarwal, once in the Episode of Satyamev Jayate Season 2[21], discussed about the use incinerators as waste management. In his discussion, he says that Incinerators should not be used for waste management as its release Dioxin in the air that is very dangerous for the health as well as for the environment. Moreover, the Incinerators are very costly for the waste management. So some alternative methods should be used in place of Incinerators.

4. CONSTITUTIONAL RIGHTS FOR SAFE ENVIRONMENT AND JUDGEMENTS

From the above discussion we noticed that most of the Medical Institution they are not following the guidelines given under The Bio-Medical Waste (Management and Handling) Rules, 1998. They used to dumped their biomedical waste at any place without taking the precautions or giving treatments to biomedical waste, which is a great violation of The Bio-Medical Waste (Management and Handling) Rules and also to the fundamental rights granted under Article 21, "Right to life under Protection of life and personal liberty[22]", Article 48A which grants " Protection and improvement of environment and safeguarding of forests and wild life[23]", and Article 51(g) which says

---

[20] Id. Para 11
[21] "Reduce, Recycle, Reuse says Satyamev Jayate", India Opines
http://indiaopines.com/reduce-recycle-reuse-satyamev-jayate/(accessed, August 30, 2014)

[22] V.N.Shukla, "Constitution of India",(Lucknow: Eastern law Company,2006),164.
[23] Ibid.312

that it should be the fundamental duty of every citizen" to protect and improve the national environment including forests, lakes, rivers and wild life, and to have compassion for living creatures[24]".

The Supreme Court of India in several cases has pronounced landmark judgments relating to Environment pollution and its impact in the society like,In Vellore Citizens Welfare Forum vs. Union of India (1996) 5 SCC 647[25]. In this case, Court said that if any industries is involved in the manufacturing of chemical or hazardous substances, and such industries is required for the development of economic growth, then in that case, it can set up it. But precautionary measures should be taken for safety of the society or to reduce the risk of hazards if any, so that it should not cause any harm to the environment as well to the health of the peoples. Such industry must be located in such a place where there will be less harm to the people in case of any accident. Thus, If a industry involved in the production of hazardous substance, in that case, the more the hazardous substance will be, the more precaution should be taken by the industry.

Again, Supreme Court in Subhas Kumar versus State of Bihar, AIR 1991 SC 420[26], says that it is the right of the people under Article 21 to have pollution free air.

Even in a case, Intellectuals Forum, Tirupathi versus State of Andhra Pradesh, AIR 2006 SC 1350[27], Court says that, one cannot give permission to construct any industries for the sake of development of the country or a state by destroying the ecological resources.

5. SUGGESTION

> - Strict rule and punishment should be imposed for the hospitals authority, who violates the rule given under The Bio-Medical Waste (Management and Handling) Rules, 1998.
> - It should be compulsory for the hospitals authority to give the vaccine of Hepatitis B and C injection to its staff free of cost, so that they should not suffered from Hepatitis B and C while handling the biomedical waste.

---

[24] Ibid.314
[25] P.M. Bakshi,"The Constitution of India", 12th Edn., Pocket Size Edition(New Delhi: Universal Law Publishing Co.Pvt.Ltd.,2013),59.
[26] Ibid.
[27] Ibid.109

➢ The process of Incineration should not be used, as this process is harmful and cause environment pollution. In place of Incineration some other process should be used which will be environment friendly like.

➢ The sharps should be stored in the medicated unbreakable, sealed container after giving treatment, for its dumping, as it will be safe for other peoples like hospitals authority, rag pickers etc who handles such kind of waste management.

➢ The remaining bottom ash from the incineration should be placed or stored in airtight sealed medicated container and after that, should be buried deeply.

➢ The media can play a vital role for spreading message for biomedical and municipal waste management and its hazards if not handled properly.

➢ The Government should give training and education to rag pickers, so that they would be able to know about the proper way of handling and management of different wastes and about the biomedical hazards symbols and its importance in biomedical waste management. They should be provided with gloves, mask and shoes which can protect them from germs, sharps materials etc.

➢ In addition, the hospitals authority should provide hand gloves, germs free suit, shoes etc to its staff also, who deals the management of biomedical waste. The most important thing is that they should give training to its staff first, for the proper handling of biomedical waste.

➢ Government can pass law, for giving training and education for all those people including hospitals staffs who regularly deal with different kinds of waste management.

➢ Government should motivate all the Hospitals and to the other peoples of the society to minimize the production of the waste and to handle and dumped this waste with proper care.

➢ The Central government should pass new rule where by asking each state government to check that whether every hospitals or any other medical institution in there state were following the guidelines of The Bio-Medical Waste (Management and Handling) Rules, 1998 or not. In addition, they have to submit report quarterly to the Central Environment ministry about the same like quantity of biomedical waste produced by each Hospital and how they treated it and name of the staff who were handling it and the area where they dumped it.

> The Government should motivate the Biotechnology students to invent new technology/methods for Environment friendly biomedical waste management.

> Even a law may be passed, whereby no authorized person including the rag pickers will be allowed to enter into the dumped area and nobody should be allowed to stay near to place of dumped area. And falling of which will be a criminal offence with fine.

> Then program like Satyamev Jayate[28] host by Amir Khan should be shown more in the television for spreading awareness in the society about the waste management.

> Like other Countries e.g. Dubai, here in India the Government should imposed fine to person who thrown garbage/waste in road or any other place other then garbage bin.

> The biomedical waste products, which are made of plastics, can be used to prepare road by using the technique invented by Dr. R Vasudevan of Thyagrajan College of Engneering[29].

> The Government should take some steps for the improvement of the work condition, health and the life of the rag pickers. As they also work for the benefit of the society by picking waste from the society. In addition, Government should provide them the Vaccine for Hepatitis B and C.

---

[28] Satyamev Jayate Season 2,"Don't Waste your Garbage" Episode 3, 15 March 2014, http://www.satyamevjayate.in/dont-waste-your-garbage.aspx, (accessed August 28, 2014)
[29] "Reduce, Recycle, Reuse says Satyamev Jayate", India Opines http://indiaopines.com/reduce-recycle-reuse-satyamev-jayate/(accessed, August 30, 2014)

6. CONCLUSIONS

If we want to live in a society, which will be free from pollution, then it should be our responsibility to keep it clean. Government is there to protect our rights and to punish the culprit who violates its rule. We should not blame the Government always for the miss happening in the society either its relate to crime or of environment pollution. Government can makes rules and regulations for us for our benefit and it should be our responsibility to follow that rules and regulation then only we can develop and if we develop then our country will develop. So it should be our duty to check that whether the guidelines given by The Bio-Medical Waste (Management and Handling) Rules, 1998 is followed by every medical institution or not. We visit medicals only when we are sick, and the responsibility of the doctors is to treat us. So it is also our duty to enquire whether they are following the guidelines or not. Ultimately, it will be, we only who will suffer from the pollution created from the biomedical medical waste. The day when we will start asked question about the guidelines for the dumping and treatment of the Biomedical Waste management to the Hospital Authority, they would be bound to answer us and to follow the guidelines. We can use a formula to make our environment free of pollution from biomedical waste. And we can denote this formula as "W3". But for this we have to know the law and our rights first.

W3 means:-

1) Whether the hospitals authorities follow the rules The Bio-Medical Waste (Management and Handling) Rules, 1998 for the treatment and management of biomedical waste?

2) Whether the people who are engaged for the handling of waste were trained to handle the biomedical waste?

3) Whether the hospitals authority provides all the important things like gloves, shoes, germs free cloth to their staff for handling the biomedical waste?

This three simple question can change our life's including the environment.